Spell with Zip

Zip

Zip is a friendly space alien from planet Zee. He loves to learn. Zip uses his hands to speak to his friends. He can't wait to teach the people of planet Earth all about sign language. Zip is the captain of his spaceship.

Pella

Pella is Zip's best friend. She also comes from planet Zee. Pella is very brave. Although she is a little younger than Zip and Statz, she isn't afraid of anything and is always the first of the three friends to try new things.

Statz

Statz is in charge of computers on the spaceship. He loves gadgets. Statz uses his Zablet to help him and his friends out of sticky situations. He is excited to learn about planet Earth and all the people who live here.

Goober

Goober is an unexpected guest on the friends' adventures. A greedy and naughty space stowaway, Goober has the ability to change his colour and shape so is always jumping out and surprising Zip, Pella and Statz.

Zip's top tips

Zip and friends are here to help you talk in a fun new way - spell with your fingers and talk with your hands. Follow these top tips to get the most from their adventures:

- **Share the book together and enjoy the story**
- **Play with the signs**
- **Use Zip's alphabet to make your own words**
- **Visit Space School, enjoy the activities and have fun**
- **Watch out for Goober...**

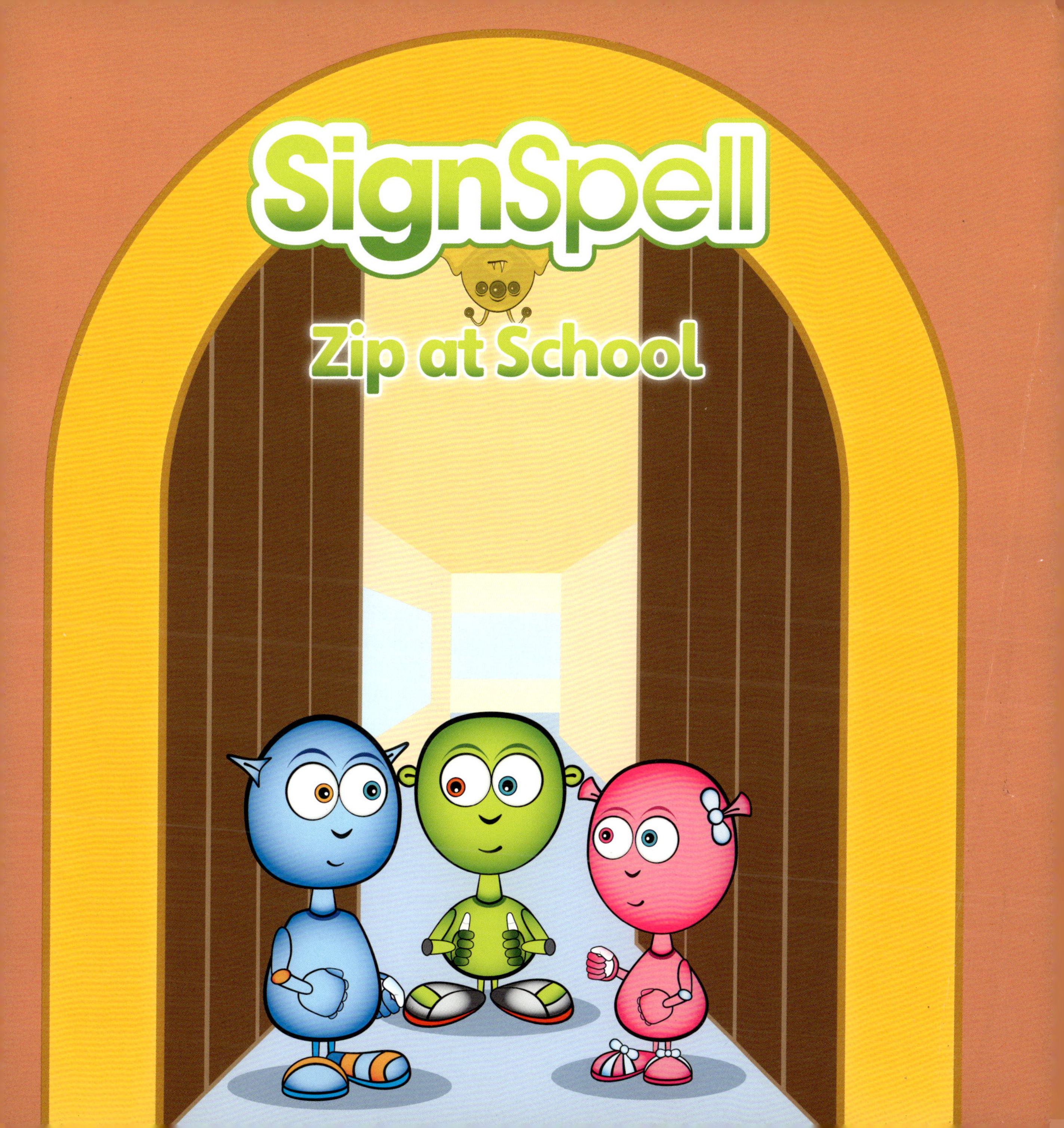
SignSpell
Zip at School

The spaceship has landed in a playground. Zip, Pella and Statz can't wait to find out how humans learn on planet Earth.

A friendly-looking teacher is ringing a bell to call everyone into the school. "Good morning," she calls, as they all file into their lessons.

Ring, Ring,
Ring, Ring,

On planet Zee, everyone learns together in one very big class and there is a different school for every subject. They go to a different school each day.

Zip, Pella and Statz love the Lingo Space School where they learn languages from across the galaxies.

The first lesson for the friends is maths.
They each find a desk in their new classroom and sit down.

Statz already knows his times tables back to front. “Brilliant,” he says.
“I love sums, I hope we get some for homework.”

Zip and Pella like numbers too. "Me too," Pella says. "We can find some practice sums on the Zablet and test each other later."

The 2 Times Table	The 3 Times Table	The 4 Times Table	[illegible]	[illegible]
1 x 2 = 2	1 x 3 = 3	1 x 4 = 4	[illegible]	[illegible]
2 x 2 = 4	2 x 3 = 6	2 x 4 = 8	[illegible]	[illegible]
3 x 2 = 6	3 x 3 = 9	3 x 4 = 12	3 x 5 = 15	3 x 6 = 18
4 x 2 = 8	4 x 3 = 12	4 x 4 = 16	4 x 5 = 20	4 x 6 = 24
5 x 2 = 10	5 x 3 = 15	5 x 4 = 20	5 x 5 = 25	5 x 6 = 30
6 x 2 = 12	6 x 3 = 18	6 x 4 = 24	6 x 5 = 30	6 x 6 = 36
7 x 2 = 14	7 x 3 = 21	7 x 4 = 28	7 x 5 = 35	7 x 6 = 42
8 x 2 = 16	8 x 3 = 24	8 x 4 = 32	8 x 5 = 40	8 x 6 = 48
9 x 2 = 18	9 x 3 = 27	9 x 4 = 36	9 x 5 = 45	9 x 6 = 54
10 x 2 = 20	10 x 3 = 30	10 x 4 = 40	10 x 5 = 50	10 x 6 = 60
[illegible]	11 x 3 = 33	11 x 4 = 44	11 x 5 = 55	11 x 6 = 66
[illegible]	12 x 3 = 36	12 x 4 = 48	12 x 5 = 60	12 x 6 = 72

For the next lesson the whole class moves to a special science classroom.
The teacher tells everyone to put on safety jackets and goggles.
"We look like real scientists," says Pella. "I wonder what we have to do today."

The teacher gives everyone an experiment kit
and starts to write instructions on the whiteboard.

“Please read the instructions on the board before starting your experiment,” the teacher says.

Zip can’t wait to get started. He takes a green liquid out of the kit and mixes it with some orange powder.

The teacher sees Zip. “Stop!” he says alarmed, but it is too late.

The mixture starts to froth and splutter. It spills out of the container and soon the classroom is filled with bubbles.

"See what happens when you don't follow instructions, Zip?" says the teacher.

"I'm sorry," he says. "I won't do that again."

Pella and Statz offer to help Zip clean up the mess.

Space School

Take a look at the pictures; you may have seen them in the story.
See if you can spell each one using Zip's alphabet.

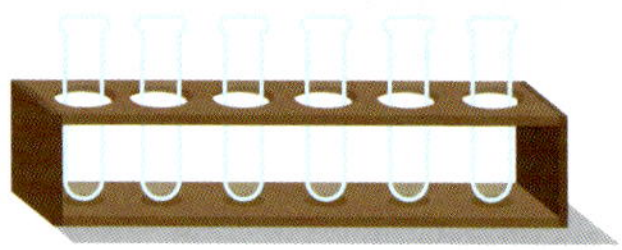

It doesn't take long for the friends to pop all the bubbles and clear away the slime they leave everywhere. Zip cleans all the desks with a cloth, Pella mops the floor and Statz wipes all the containers.

When the classroom is clean, Zip writes all about the experiment in his exercise book.

Book

The last lesson of the day is art. Pella loves drawing and painting.

“Today we are all going to paint a picture of an alien from another planet,” says the teacher. “In the cupboard you will find all the paints, crayons and colouring pens you need.”

Zip, Pella and Statz rush to the cupboard to get paints and paintbrushes.

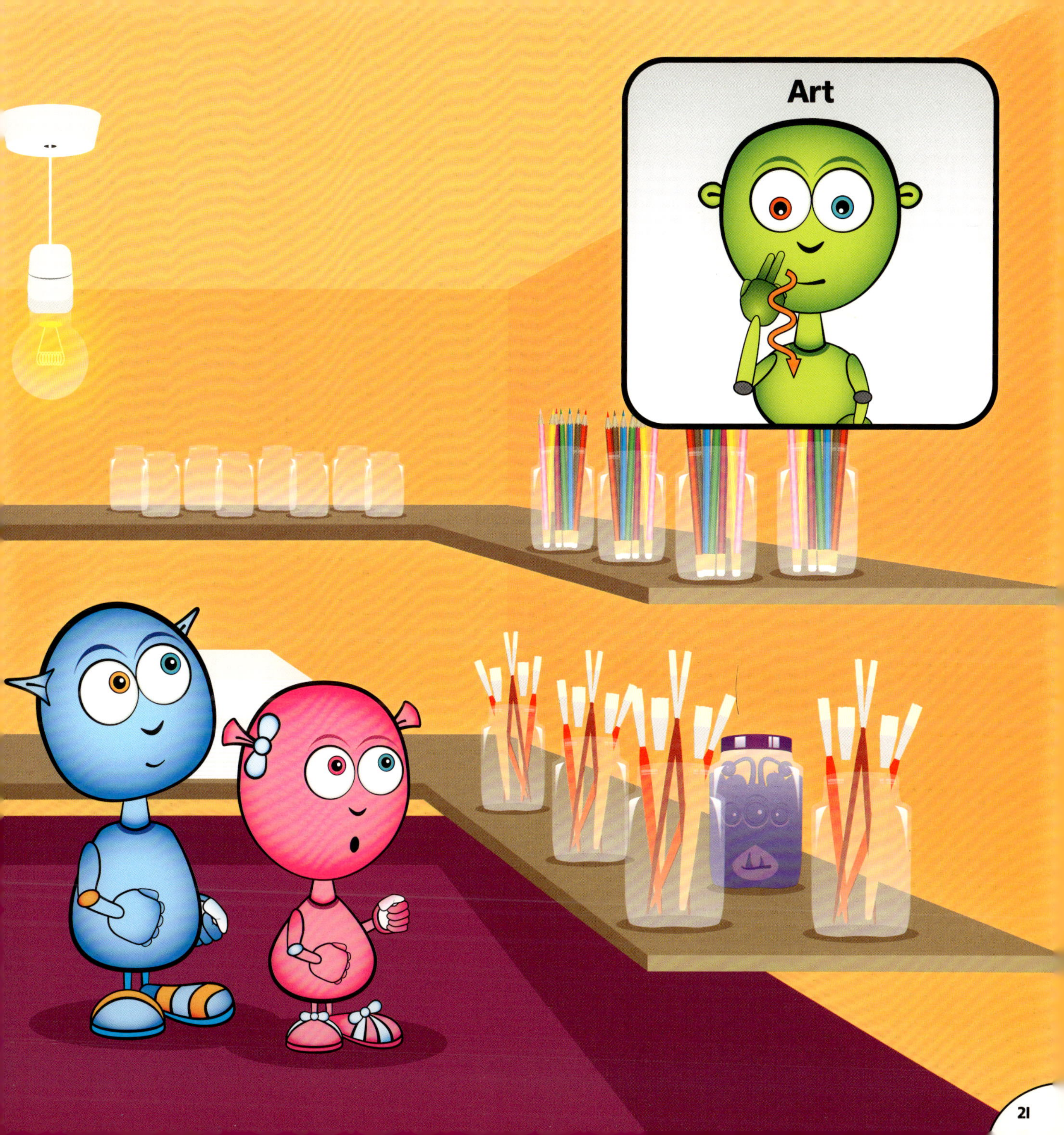
Art

The whole class is very quiet as they concentrate on their aliens. When everyone is finished the teacher carefully picks up each painting and pins it to the wall.

"Wow, look at all these aliens," says Zip.
"I wonder which planets they are from?"

"I think our aliens look the funniest!" laughs Pella.

"We've all painted humans," says Statz. "I wonder if the teacher will count them as aliens here on planet Earth!"

The teacher takes a long look at each painting.
“This one is good,” she says. “This one is great too.”

"I'm very proud of you all," she tells the class.
"You have worked very hard indeed."

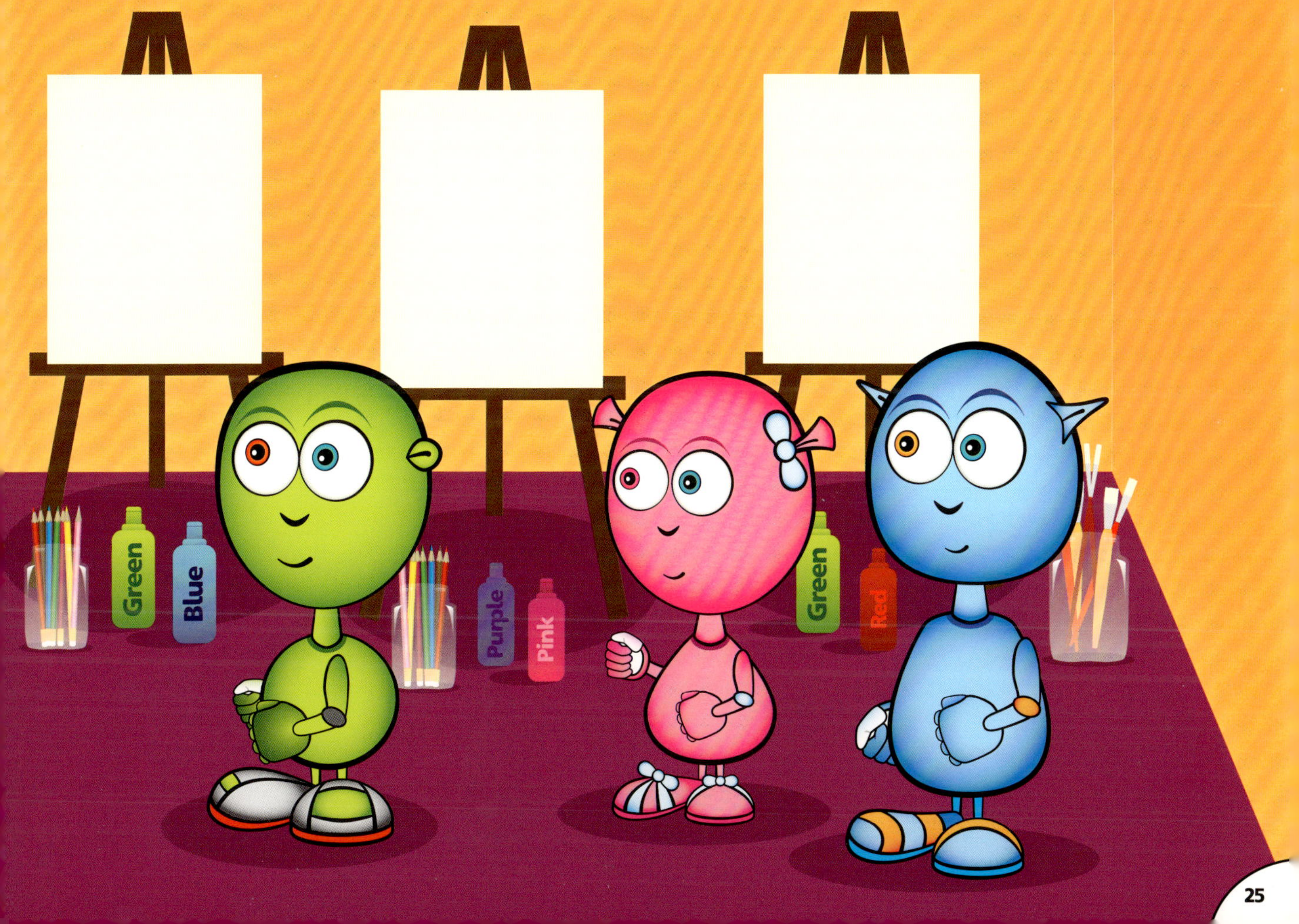

Space School

Zip is enjoying his first day at school. Can you see some of the words you have learnt to sign from the story? See if you can remember how to sign them.

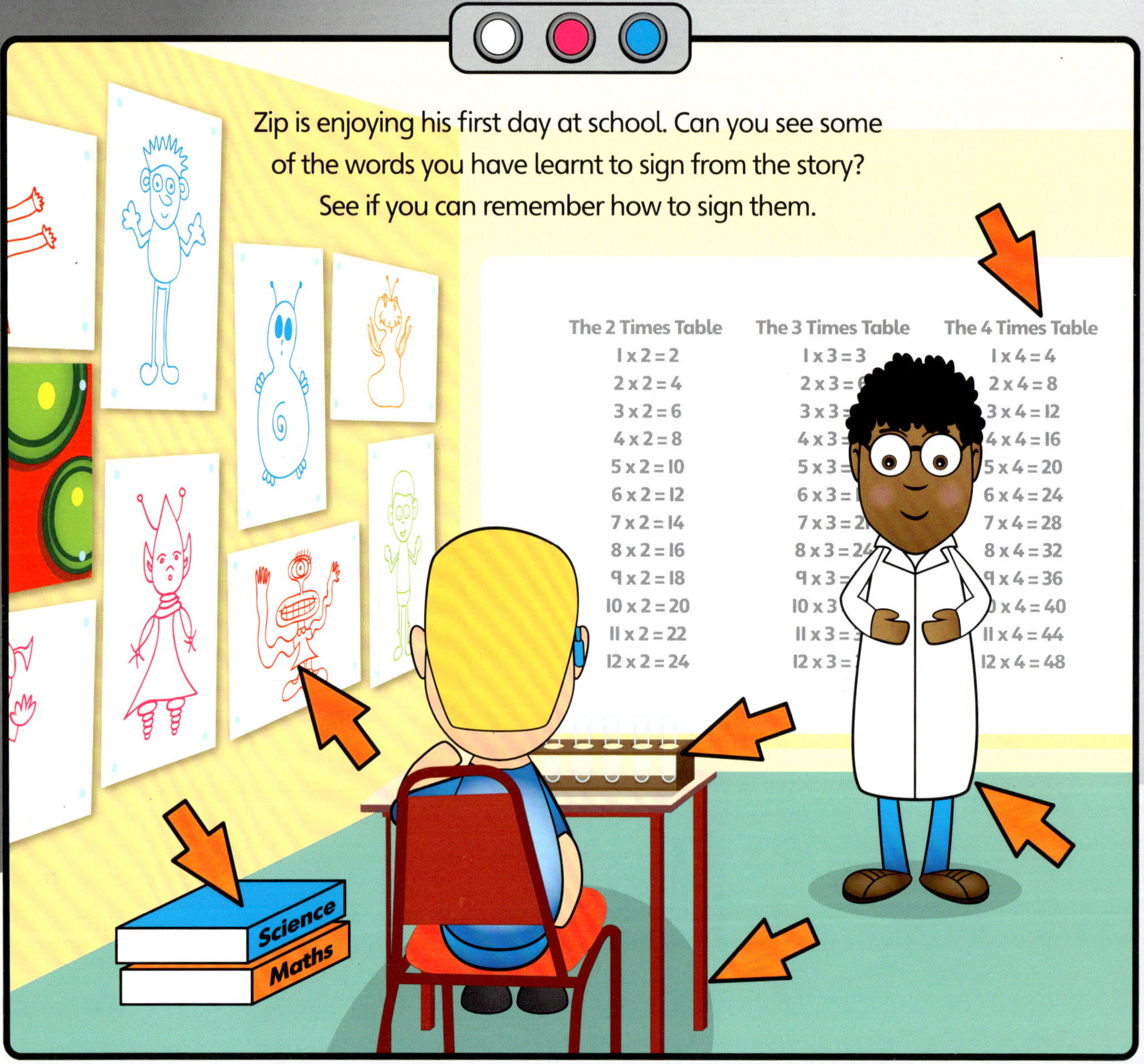

"The alien in this painting is very, very good," she says. "It looks so real!"

She puts a star on the painting and holds it up for everyone to see. "This is my favourite," she says.

"Aaagh, it moved," she shouts. "What is it?"

Goober
Pink

Zip's Signs

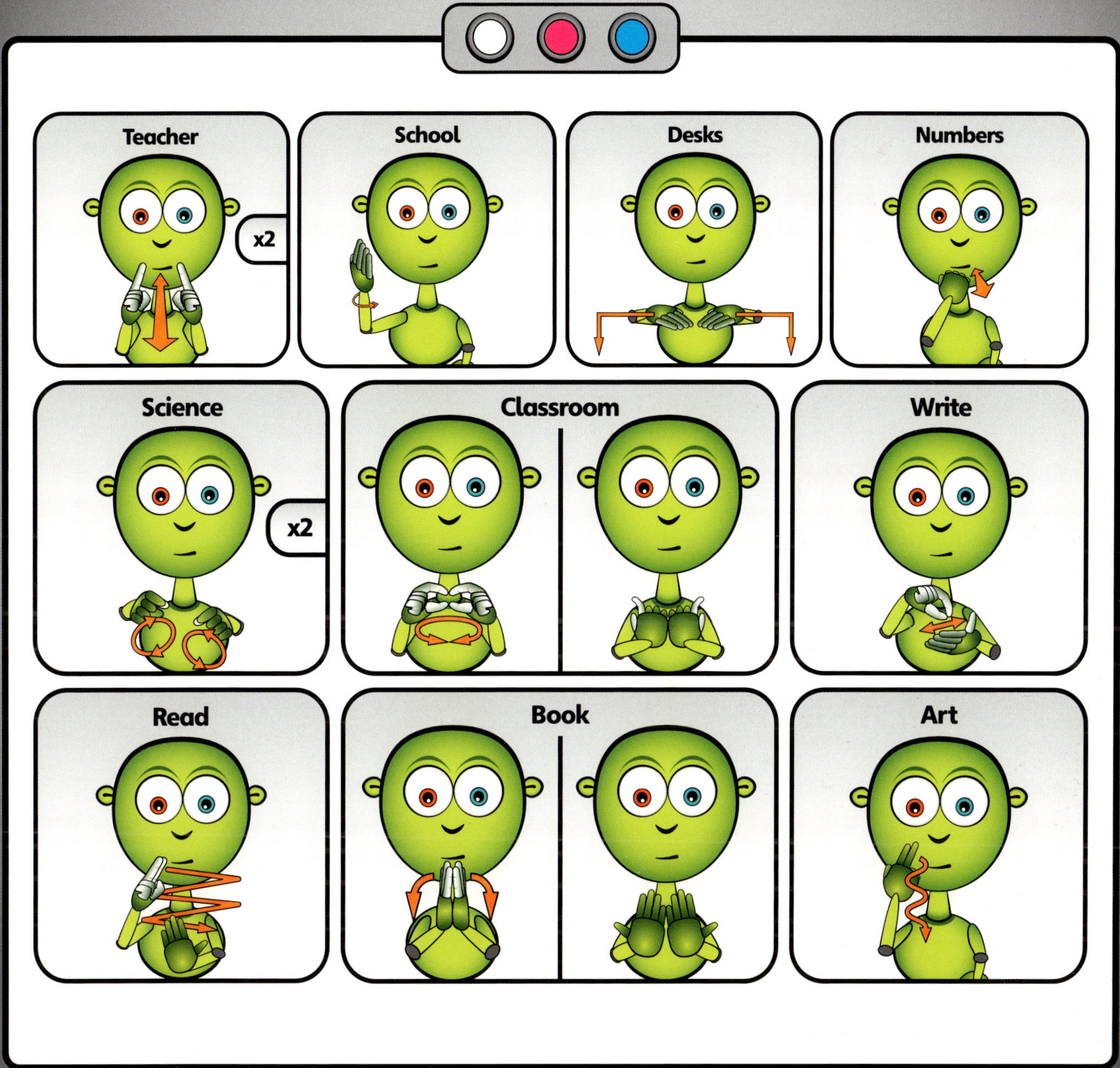
Teacher
x2
School
Desks
Numbers
Science
x2
Classroom
Write
Read
Book
Art

Fun things to do

Now that you have read all about Zip at School,
here are some fun things for you to do:

- **Draw or paint your own space alien picture**
- **Plan your perfect day at school. What lessons would you have?**
- **What would you do if your classroom got covered in bubbles?**
- **How did you feel on your first day at school?**
- **What Space Schools would there be on planet Zee?**
- **Teach a friend how to spell the name of their favourite teacher**

First published 2013 by Signature

SignSpell® stories created by Signature
Designed and illustrated by Igloo Imaging Ltd.